TYPE 1 DIABETES COOKBOOK FOR MEN

The Complete Dietitian-Approved Low Carb and Mouth-watering Guide with Tasty, Quick And Easy Healthy Recipes (14-Day Meal Plan Included)

Lisa R. Ashley

Copyright © 2023 by Lisa R. Ashley

The contents of the book, including any text or images, may not be reproduced in any form or by any means, such as photocopying or recording, without written permission from the publisher. This also indicates that the book is protected by copyright and that the copyright is held by Lisa R. Ashley

Table of Contents

Introduction

Chapter 1: Diabetes-Friendly Basics
- **Carbohydrate Counting Made Easy**
- **Glycemic Index and Load**

Chapter 2: Ten(10) Delicious Breakfast Recipes

Chapter 3: Ten(10) Satisfying Lunch Recipes

Chapter 4: Ten(10) Mouth-watering Dinner Recipes

Chapter 5: Ten (10) Easy to Prepare Snacks and Treats Recipes

Chapter 6: Meal Planning Tips and Tricks
14-Day Meal plan
- **Day 1:**
- **Day 2:**
- **Day 3:**
- **Day 4:**

- Day 5:
- Day 6:
- Day 7:
- Day 8:
- Day 9:
- Day 10:
- Day 11:
- Day 12:
- Day 13:
- Day 14:

Conclusion

- Putting It All Together: A Balanced Approach to Type 1
- Staying Motivated and Inspired

If you ever come across any question concerning the recipes in this book, you can reach me via email. I will be more than happy to assist you.

Lisaashley623@gmail.com

Introduction

Robert, a 40-year-old man, was leading a fulfilling life in a bustling city. He was known for his vibrant personality, active lifestyle, and strong work ethic. However, his life took an unexpected turn when he started experiencing a series of puzzling symptoms.

Robert noticed that he was losing weight rapidly, felt constant fatigue, and had an unquenchable thirst that seemed insatiable. Concerned about his deteriorating health, he decided to seek medical advice and made an appointment with me.

Walking into my office, Robert couldn't help but feel a mix of anxiety and anticipation. He described his symptoms and shared his worries about his declining well-being. I carefully listened to Robert's concerns and decided to conduct a thorough examination and a series of tests.

Days later, he returned to my office to learn the results. The atmosphere in the room was filled with tension as he sat on the edge of his seat, waiting for me to deliver the news. With a gentle smile, I began to explain the diagnosis—I diagnosed him with Type 1 diabetes.

Overwhelmed by the news, he struggled to process the reality of living with a chronic condition. I, aware of the emotional impact, reassured him that with proper management, he could lead a fulfilling life. I emphasised the significance of adopting a tailored diet plan to regulate his blood sugar levels effectively.

I patiently explained the importance of understanding carbohydrates, monitoring blood sugar levels, and making healthy food choices. I worked closely with Robert, answering his questions and addressing his concerns, ensuring that he felt supported and empowered to manage his condition.

Leaving the clinic that day, Robert's mind buzzed with a mix of emotions—fear, determination, and hope. He was determined to embrace his new reality and take control of his health. Armed with the diet plan provided by me, he embarked on a journey of self-discovery and adaptation.

Day by day, Robert implemented the dietary guidelines, making mindful choices that supported his overall well-being. He learned to monitor his blood sugar levels diligently, adjusting his insulin doses accordingly. As he educated himself about Type 1 diabetes, he realised that managing his condition was not just about the food he consumed but also about leading a balanced and healthy lifestyle.

Robert's commitment and resilience paid off. Over time, he found a rhythm in managing his blood sugar levels, making adjustments to his diet and insulin regimen as needed. He discovered a newfound appreciation for his body and its resilience, realising that with the right mindset and support, he could live a vibrant and fulfilling life, even with Type 1 diabetes.

Robert's journey inspired those around him. His positive attitude and unwavering determination served as a beacon of hope for others facing similar challenges. He became an advocate for diabetes awareness, sharing his story and supporting those in need.

While Type 1 diabetes was an uninvited guest in Robert's life, he transformed it into an opportunity for growth, resilience, and compassion. Through effective management and the support of my guidance, Robert showed the world that a diagnosis is not an end but a beginning—a chance to rise above and embrace life's challenges with grace and courage.

Are you ready to achieve even more success in eating better than Robert? Let's proceed.

You got this!

Chapter 1: Diabetes-Friendly Basics

Carbohydrate Counting Made Easy

Carbohydrate counting is an important ability for men with type 1 diabetes since it enables precise meal planning and insulin administration. Here's a step-by-step strategy to efficiently counting carbohydrates:

1. Recognize Carbohydrates' Role: Carbohydrates are the primary foodstuff responsible for rising blood sugar levels. They are turned down into glucose when ingested, which enters the bloodstream and impacts blood sugar levels. To properly manage your blood sugar, you must first understand the effects of carbohydrates on your body.

2. Recognize Carbohydrate Sources:

Learn about the common sources of carbs in your diet. Grains (rice, pasta, bread), starchy vegetables (potatoes, maize, peas), fruits, dairy products, legumes, and sugary foods (sweets, desserts) are examples of these. Reading product labels and other credible information will assist you in accurately identifying carbohydrate-containing items.

3. Measure Portion Sizes: It is critical to accurately measure portion sizes when calculating carbohydrates. To achieve precise measurements, use measuring cups, kitchen scales, or other instruments. This phase is especially critical for carbohydrate-rich foods like rice, pasta, and cereal, where portion sizes can vary greatly.

4. Consult Carbohydrate Reference Guides: Whether in print or digital form, carbohydrate reference guides give complete lists of foods and their carbohydrate content. These resources allow you to easily search for the amount of carbohydrates in various foods, making meal

planning easier. Smartphone apps created exclusively for carbohydrate counting can also be useful.

5. Calculate Carbohydrate value: Once you've determined the carbohydrate value of each food item, sum the carbs in your meal. To calculate the total carbohydrate content, add the carbs from each dietary component. Keep an eye out for hidden carbs, such as those found in sauces, dressings, or condiments.

6. Take into account the Glycemic Index: The glycemic index (GI) assesses how rapidly carbohydrates in a food elevate blood sugar levels. While not required for carbohydrate counting, understanding the GI can help you make better decisions. Low GI foods release glucose more slowly, resulting in a more consistent blood sugar response. This is especially useful when dealing with post-meal blood sugar rises.

7. Monitor and Adjust: After each meal, check your blood sugar levels to see how well your carbohydrate counting and insulin dosing are in sync. You will

gradually have a better knowledge of how different foods and portion amounts affect your blood sugar levels. Make modifications and improve your carbohydrate counting skills using this knowledge.

Glycemic Index and Load

The Glycemic Index (GI) and Glycemic Load (GL) are two key concepts in the study of carbohydrates and their effect on blood sugar levels. Understanding these parameters can help men with type 1 diabetes manage their blood glucose more successfully. Let's take a closer look at the Glycemic Index and Glycemic Load:

The Glycemic Index (GI) is a numerical scale that assesses carbohydrates based on their ability to elevate blood sugar levels when compared to a reference food, often pure glucose or white bread. Each food is assigned a value based on how quickly or slowly it raises blood sugar levels. Foods with a high GI are swiftly digested and absorbed, resulting in a more rapid rise in blood glucose levels, whereas foods with a low GI are digested more slowly, resulting in a more gradual rise in blood sugar.

The following is a breakdown of the GI categories:

- Low GI (55 or less): Most fruits and vegetables, legumes, and whole grains such as oats and barley are examples.
- Medium GI (56-69): Whole wheat products, basmati rice, and sweet potatoes fall into this category.
- High GI (70 or higher): White bread, white rice, processed cereals, and sugary beverages are examples.

Glycemic Load (GL): While the GI indicates how particular foods affect blood sugar, it does not take into account the amount of carbohydrates taken. The Glycemic Load comes into play here. The Glycemic Load considers both the quality and quantity of carbs in a given dietary portion. It is computed by multiplying a food's GI by its carbohydrate content and dividing the result by 100.

The following is a breakdown of the GL categories:
- Low GL (10 or less): Consuming these foods has little effect on blood sugar levels.
- Medium GL (11-19): These foods may have a minor impact on blood sugar levels.

- High GL (20 or higher): These foods can produce a large increase in blood sugar levels.

Because it takes into account the amount of carbs consumed, the Glycemic Load is thought to be a more useful metric than the GI alone. It assists men in understanding the total influence of a specific diet on blood glucose levels.

Understanding the Glycemic Index and Load: Understanding the GI and GL of foods can help men with type 1 diabetes manage their blood sugar levels. Low GI and GL foods are often advised because they cause a slower, more steady rise in blood sugar, which aids in maintaining stable glucose management. Individual responses to foods might vary, and factors such as meal composition, portion sizes, and other dietary components can all influence blood glucose levels.

In practice, men with type 1 diabetes can combine GI and GL knowledge into meal planning by:

1. Eat a mix of nutritious grains, fruits, vegetables, legumes, and lean proteins to lower your GI and GL.
2. Balance high GI foods: When eating high GI foods, couple them with low GI foods or incorporate sources of protein and healthy fats to aid reduce glucose absorption.
3. Regularly test your blood glucose levels before and after meals to see how different foods and their GI/GL affect your specific reaction.
4. Consultation with healthcare professionals: Consult with a certified dietitian or diabetic educator who can provide individualised advice based on your specific needs, taking the GI/GL and other considerations into account.

Remember that, while the GI and GL can provide useful information, they are only one component of a total diabetes care approach.

Chapter 2: Breakfast Recipes

When it comes to managing type 1 diabetes, it's important to focus on a balanced diet that includes a variety of nutrient-rich foods. Here are 10 breakfast foods suitable for men with type 1 diabetes:

Scrambled eggs with vegetables (spinach, bell peppers, mushrooms):

Ingredients:
- 2 large eggs
- 1/4 cup spinach, chopped
- 1/4 cup bell peppers, diced
- 1/4 cup mushrooms, sliced
- Salt and pepper to taste
- Cooking oil or butter for the pan

Instructions:

1. Heat a non-stick skillet over medium heat and add a small amount of cooking oil or butter.
2. Whisk the eggs together with pepper and salt in a small bowl.
3. Add the chopped spinach, diced bell peppers, and sliced mushrooms to the skillet and cook until the vegetables are tender.
4. Pour the whisked eggs into the skillet with the cooked vegetables and stir gently with a spatula.
5. Continue cooking and stirring the eggs until they reach your desired level of doneness.
6. Remove from heat and serve hot.

Nutritional Information:

The nutritional content of scrambled eggs with vegetables may vary based on the specific quantities used and cooking methods. Here is a general approximation per serving:

- Calories: around 200-250
- Protein: around 12-15 grams
- Fat: around 14-18 grams

- Carbohydrates: around 8-10 grams
- Fibre: around 2-3 grams

Whole grain toast with avocado and sliced turkey:

Ingredients:
- 2 slices of whole grain bread
- 1 ripe avocado, mashed
- 4-6 slices of turkey breast
- Salt and pepper to taste

Instructions:
1. Toast the slices of whole grain bread to your desired level of crispiness.
2. Spread the mashed avocado evenly on each slice of toast.
3. Layer the turkey slices on top of the avocado.
4. Season with salt and pepper according to your taste preferences.

5. Serve and enjoy.

Nutritional Information:

The nutritional content of whole grain toast with avocado and sliced turkey may vary depending on the specific brands and quantities used. Here is a general approximation per serving:

- Calories: around 300-350
- Protein: around 20-25 grams
- Fat: around 10-15 grams
- Carbohydrates: around 30-35 grams
- Fibre: around 8-10 grams

Greek yoghourt with berries and a sprinkle of nuts

Ingredients:
- 1 cup Greek yoghourt
- Assorted berries (e.g., strawberries, blueberries, raspberries)

- A handful of nuts (e.g., almonds, walnuts, or pistachios)

Instructions:

1. Spoon the Greek yoghurt into a bowl.
2. Wash and prepare the berries by rinsing them under water.
3. Add the assorted berries on top of the Greek yoghurt.
4. Sprinkle a handful of nuts over the berries.
5. Enjoy as is or drizzle with honey for added sweetness (optional).

Nutritional Information:

The nutritional content of Greek yoghurt with berries and nuts can vary based on the specific brands and quantities used. Here is a general approximation per serving:

- Calories: around 200-250
- Protein: around 15-20 grams
- Fat: around 5-10 grams
- Carbohydrates: around 20-25 grams
- Fibre: around 3-5 grams

Oatmeal made with water or unsweetened almond milk, topped with cinnamon and sliced almonds:

Ingredients:
- 1/2 cup oats (rolled oats or steel-cut oats)
- 1 cup water or unsweetened almond milk
- 1/4 teaspoon cinnamon
- 1 tablespoon sliced almonds

Instructions:
1. In a small saucepan, bring the almond milk or water to a boil.
2. Add the oats to the boiling liquid and reduce the heat to medium-low.
3. Cook the oats according to the package instructions (usually around 5-10 minutes for rolled oats, or longer for steel-cut oats), stirring occasionally.
4. Once the oats are cooked to your desired consistency, remove from heat.

5. Sprinkle cinnamon on top of the oatmeal.

6. Garnish with sliced almonds.

7. Serve hot.

Nutritional Information:

The nutritional content of oatmeal with cinnamon and sliced almonds may vary depending on the specific brands and quantities used. Here is a general approximation per serving:

- Calories: around 150-200

- Protein: around 5-7 grams

- Fat: around 4-6 grams

- Carbohydrates: around 25-30 grams

- Fibre: around 4-6 grams

Veggie omelette with egg whites or whole eggs and mixed vegetables

Ingredients:
- 2-3 eggs or 4 egg whites
- Assorted mixed vegetables (e.g., onions, tomatoes, spinach, mushrooms, bell peppers)
- Salt and pepper to taste
- Cooking oil or butter for the pan

Instructions:

1. Heat a non-stick skillet over medium heat and add a small amount of cooking oil or butter.
2. Whisk the eggs together with pepper and salt in a small bowl.
3. Chop the mixed vegetables into small pieces.
4. Add the mixed vegetables to the skillet and sauté until they are cooked to your liking.

5. Pour the whisked eggs over the cooked vegetables and cook until the eggs are set, gently lifting the edges with a spatula to allow the uncooked eggs to flow underneath.

6. Once the omelette is cooked, transfer it onto a plate and fold it in half.

7. Serve hot.

Nutritional Information:

The nutritional content of a veggie omelette can vary depending on the specific quantities and types of ingredients used. Here is a general approximation per serving:

- Calories: around 150-200
- Protein: around 12-15 grams
- Fat: around 8-10 grams
- Carbohydrates: around 5-8 grams
- Fibre: around 2-4 grams

Cottage cheese with sliced tomatoes and whole grain crackers

Ingredients:
- 1/2 cup cottage cheese
- 1 small tomato, sliced
- Whole grain crackers

Instructions:
1. Spoon the cottage cheese into a bowl.
2. Slice the tomato into thin slices.
3. Arrange the tomato slices on top of the cottage cheese.
4. Serve with whole grain crackers on the side.
5. Enjoy!

Nutritional Information:
The nutritional content of cottage cheese with sliced tomatoes and whole grain crackers can vary based on the specific brands and quantities used. Here is a general approximation per serving:
- Calories: around 150-200

- Protein: around 15-20 grams
- Fat: around 5-8 grams
- Carbohydrates: around 10-15 grams
- Fibre: around 2-4 grams

Smoothie made with unsweetened almond milk, spinach, berries, and a scoop of protein powder

Ingredients:
- 1 cup unsweetened almond milk
- Handful of spinach leaves
- Assorted berries (e.g., strawberries, blueberries, raspberries)
- 1 scoop of protein powder (flavour of your choice)

Instructions:
1. In a blender, combine the unsweetened almond milk, spinach, berries, and protein powder.
2. Blend until smooth and well combined.

3. If desired, add ice cubes to make the smoothie colder and more refreshing.

4. Pour into a glass and enjoy.

Nutritional Information:

The nutritional content of a smoothie can vary depending on the specific brands and quantities used. Here is a general approximation per serving:

- Calories: around 200-250
- Protein: around 20-25 grams
- Fat: around 5-8 grams
- Carbohydrates: around 20-25 grams
- Fibre: around 5-8 grams

Whole grain cereal with unsweetened almond milk and a handful of walnuts

Ingredients:

- 1 cup whole grain cereal (e.g., oats, bran flakes, or whole grain flakes)

- 1 cup unsweetened almond milk
- A handful of walnuts

Instructions:

1. Pour the whole grain cereal into a bowl.
2. Add the unsweetened almond milk to the cereal.
3. Top with a handful of walnuts.
4. Enjoy!

Nutritional Information:

The nutritional content of whole grain cereal with unsweetened almond milk and walnuts can vary based on the specific brands and quantities used. Here is a general approximation per serving:

- Calories: around 200-250
- Protein: around 5-8 grams
- Fat: around 8-10 grams
- Carbohydrates: around 30-35 grams
- Fibre: around 5-8 grams

Low-fat cottage cheese mixed with diced fruits:

Ingredients:
- 1/2 cup low-fat cottage cheese
- Assorted diced fruits (e.g., apples, berries, bananas, or oranges)

Instructions:
1. Spoon the low-fat cottage cheese into a bowl.
2. Dice the fruits into small pieces.
3. Add the diced fruits to the cottage cheese.
4. Mix well to combine.
5. Serve and enjoy.

Nutritional Information:
The nutritional content of low-fat cottage cheese mixed with diced fruits can vary based on the specific quantities and types of fruits used. Here is a general approximation per serving:
- Calories: around 100-150

- Protein: around 10-15 grams
- Fat: around 1-3 grams
- Carbohydrates: around 15-20 grams
- Fibre: around 2-4 grams

Smoked salmon with whole grain bagel and cream cheese:

Ingredients:
- 2 slices of smoked salmon
- 1 whole grain bagel
- Cream cheese (optional)
- Sliced red onion (optional)
- Capers (optional)
- Fresh dill (optional)

Instructions:
1. Slice the whole grain bagel in half.
2. Spread cream cheese on each half of the bagel (if desired).

3. Place a slice of smoked salmon on each half of the bagel.

4. If desired, top with sliced red onion, capers, and fresh dill for added flavour.

5. Serve and enjoy.

Nutritional Information:

The nutritional content of smoked salmon with a whole grain bagel and cream cheese can vary based on the specific brands and quantities used. Here is a general approximation per serving:

- Calories: around 300-400
- Protein: around 15-20 grams
- Fat: around 10-15 grams
- Carbohydrates: around 35-40 grams
- Fibre: around 5-8 grams

Please note that the nutritional information provided is an estimate and can vary depending on the specific ingredients and brands used.

Chapter 3: Satisfying Lunch Recipes

When planning a lunch for someone with type 1 diabetes, it's important to focus on foods that promote stable blood sugar levels and provide balanced nutrition. Here are ten lunch food options that can be suitable for men with type 1 diabetes:

Grilled chicken breast salad

Ingredients:
- 4 ounces grilled chicken breast, sliced
- Mixed salad greens
- Assorted vegetables (e.g., tomatoes, cucumbers, bell peppers, carrots)
- Salad dressing of your choice (optional)

Instructions:
1. Place a bed of mixed salad greens on a plate.
2. Arrange the sliced grilled chicken breast on top of the salad greens.

3. Add the assorted vegetables to the salad.

4. Drizzle with your favourite salad dressing, if desired.

5. Toss the salad gently to combine the ingredients.

6. Serve and enjoy.

Nutritional Information:

The nutritional content of a grilled chicken breast salad can vary based on the specific quantities and types of ingredients used, as well as the dressing chosen. Here is a general approximation per serving:

- Calories: around 250-300
- Protein: around 25-30 grams
- Fat: around 10-15 grams
- Carbohydrates: around 15-20 grams
- Fibre: around 5-8 grams

Turkey lettuce wraps

Ingredients:
- Lettuce leaves (e.g., iceberg lettuce or romaine lettuce)
- 4-6 ounces cooked turkey breast, sliced
- Assorted vegetables (e.g., shredded carrots, sliced bell peppers, sliced cucumbers)
- Sauce of your choice (e.g., low-sodium soy sauce, hoisin sauce, or peanut sauce)

Instructions:
1. Wash and dry the lettuce leaves.
2. Place the cooked turkey breast slices on each lettuce leaf.
3. Add the assorted vegetables on top of the turkey.
4. Drizzle with your preferred sauce.
5. Roll up the lettuce leaves, tucking in the sides to create a wrap.
6. Serve and enjoy.

Nutritional Information:

The nutritional content of turkey lettuce wraps can vary based on the specific quantities and types of ingredients used, as well as the sauce chosen. Here is a general approximation per serving:

- Calories: around 150-200
- Protein: around 20-25 grams
- Fat: around 5-8 grams
- Carbohydrates: around 5-8 grams
- Fibre: around 2-4 grams

Quinoa and vegetable stir-fry

Ingredients:

- 1 cup cooked quinoa
- Assorted vegetables (e.g., broccoli, bell peppers, carrots, snap peas)
- 1-2 tablespoons cooking oil
- Soy sauce or teriyaki sauce for seasoning

Instructions:

1. Heat the cooking oil in a large skillet or wok over medium-high heat.

2. Add the assorted vegetables to the skillet and stir-fry until they are crisp-tender.

3. Add the cooked quinoa to the skillet and stir-fry for another minute or two to heat it through.

4. Season with soy sauce or teriyaki sauce according to your taste preferences.

5. Serve hot.

Nutritional Information:

The nutritional content of quinoa and vegetable stir-fry can vary based on the specific quantities and types of ingredients used. Here is a general approximation per serving:

- Calories: around 250-300
- Protein: around 8-10 grams
- Fat: around 8-10 grams
- Carbohydrates: around 35-40 grams
- Fibre: around 5-8 grams

Grilled salmon with roasted vegetables

Ingredients:
- 4-6 ounces grilled salmon fillet
- Assorted vegetables (e.g., broccoli, carrots, zucchini, bell peppers)
- Cooking oil
- Salt, pepper, and herbs or spices of your choice for seasoning

Instructions:
1. Preheat the oven to 400°F (200°C).
2. Toss the assorted vegetables in a bowl with a small amount of cooking oil, salt, pepper, and any desired herbs or spices.
3. Lay the vegetables in a single layer on the baking sheet.
4. Roast the vegetables in the preheated oven for 15-20 minutes or until they are tender and slightly browned.
5. Meanwhile, season the salmon fillet with salt, pepper, and any desired herbs or spices.

6. Grill the salmon fillet over medium-high heat for about 4-5 minutes per side or until it is cooked through.
7. Serve the grilled salmon with the roasted vegetables.
8. Enjoy.

Nutritional Information:

The nutritional content of grilled salmon with roasted vegetables can vary based on the specific quantities and types of ingredients used. Here is a general approximation per serving:

- Calories: around 300-400
- Protein: around 25-30 grams
- Fat: around 15-20 grams
- Carbohydrates: around 15-20 grams
- Fibre: around 5-8 grams

Lentil or bean soup:

Ingredients:
- 1 cup cooked lentils or beans (e.g., lentils, black beans, chickpeas)
- Assorted vegetables (e.g., onions, carrots, celery)
- Vegetable or chicken broth
- Herbs and spices of your choice (e.g., garlic, thyme, cumin)
- Salt and pepper to taste

Instructions:
1. In a large pot, sauté the onions, carrots, and celery until they are softened.
2. Add the cooked lentils or beans to the pot.
3. Pour enough vegetable or chicken broth into the pot to cover the ingredients.
4. Add your preferred herbs and spices for flavour.
5. Bring the soup to a boil, then reduce the heat and let it simmer for about 20-30 minutes to allow the flavours to meld together.
6. Season with salt and pepper to taste.

7. Serve hot.

Nutritional Information:

The nutritional content of lentil or bean soup can vary based on the specific quantities and types of ingredients used. Here is a general approximation per serving:

- Calories: around 200-250
- Protein: around 10-15 grams
- Fat: around 2-4 grams
- Carbohydrates: around 35-40 grams
- Fibre: around 10-15 grams

Whole grain wrap with lean protein and veggies

Ingredients:
- Whole grain wrap or tortilla
- Lean protein of your choice (e.g., grilled chicken, turkey, tofu)
- Assorted vegetables (e.g., lettuce, tomatoes, cucumbers, bell peppers)

- Sauce or dressing of your choice (optional)

Instructions:

1. Lay the whole grain wrap or tortilla flat on a clean surface.
2. Place the lean protein in the centre of the wrap.
3. Add the assorted vegetables on top of the protein.
4. Drizzle with your preferred sauce or dressing, if desired.
5. Fold the sides of the wrap inward and then roll it tightly to create a wrap.
6. Serve and enjoy.

Nutritional Information:

The nutritional content of a whole grain wrap with lean protein and veggies can vary based on the specific quantities and types of ingredients used, as well as the sauce or dressing chosen. Here is a general approximation per serving:

- Calories: around 250-300
- Protein: around 15-20 grams
- Fat: around 5-8 grams

- Carbohydrates: around 35-40 grams
- Fibre: around 5-8 grams

Vegetable omelette

Ingredients:
- 2-3 eggs or 4 egg whites
- Assorted mixed vegetables (e.g., onions, tomatoes, spinach, mushrooms, bell peppers)
- Salt and pepper to taste
- Cooking oil or butter for the pan

Instructions:
1. Heat a non-stick skillet over medium heat and add a small amount of cooking oil or butter.
2. Whisk the eggs together with pepper and salt in a small bowl.
3. Chop the mixed vegetables into small pieces.
4. Add the mixed vegetables to the skillet and sauté until they are cooked to your liking.

5. Pour the whisked eggs over the cooked vegetables and cook until the eggs are set, gently lifting the edges with a spatula to allow the uncooked eggs to flow underneath.

6. Once the omelette is cooked, transfer it onto a plate and fold it in half.

7. Serve hot.

Nutritional Information:

The nutritional content of a vegetable omelette can vary depending on the specific quantities and types of ingredients used. Here is a general approximation per serving:

- Calories: around 150-200
- Protein: around 12-15 grams
- Fat: around 8-10 grams
- Carbohydrates: around 5-8 grams
- Fibre: around 2-4 grams

Greek yoghurt with mixed berries and nuts

Ingredients:
- 1 cup Greek yoghurt
- Assorted mixed berries (e.g., strawberries, blueberries, raspberries)
- A sprinkle of nuts (e.g., almonds, walnuts)

Instructions:
1. Spoon the Greek yoghurt into a bowl.
2. Add the mixed berries on top of the yoghurt.
3. Sprinkle the nuts over the berries.
4. Serve and enjoy.

Nutritional Information:
The nutritional content of Greek yoghurt with mixed berries and nuts can vary based on the specific quantities and types of ingredients used. Here is a general approximation per serving:
- Calories: around 150-200

- Protein: around 15-20 grams
- Fat: around 5-8 grams
- Carbohydrates: around 10-15 grams
- Fibre: around 2-4 grams

Tuna or salmon salad

Ingredients:

- 4-6 ounces canned tuna or salmon (in water or oil), drained
- Assorted vegetables (e.g., celery, onions, bell peppers)
- Greek yoghurt or mayonnaise for dressing
- Lemon juice (optional)
- Salt and pepper to taste

Instructions:

1. In a bowl, flake the canned tuna or salmon with a fork.
2. Chop the assorted vegetables into small pieces.
3. Add the vegetables to the bowl with the flaked fish.
4. Add Greek yoghurt or mayonnaise to the bowl and mix well to combine.

5. If desired, squeeze lemon juice over the salad for extra flavour.

6. Season with salt and pepper to taste.

7. Serve chilled.

Nutritional Information:

The nutritional content of tuna or salmon salad can vary based on the specific quantities and types of ingredients used. Here is a general approximation per serving:

- Calories: around 150-200
- Protein: around 20-25 grams
- Fat: around 5-8 grams
- Carbohydrates: around 5-8 grams
- Fibre: around 2-4 grams

Veggie and hummus wrap

Ingredients:
- Whole grain wrap or tortilla
- Assorted vegetables (e.g., lettuce, tomatoes, cucumbers, bell peppers, shredded carrots)
- Hummus for spreading

Instructions:
1. Lay the whole grain wrap or tortilla flat on a clean surface.
2. Spread a generous amount of hummus evenly over the wrap.
3. Add the assorted vegetables on top of the hummus.
4. Roll up the wrap tightly, tucking in the sides as you go.
5. Slice the wrap in half if desired.
6. Serve and enjoy.

Nutritional Information:
The nutritional content of a veggie and hummus wrap can vary based on the specific quantities and types of

ingredients used. Here is a general approximation per serving:
- Calories: around 200-250
- Protein: around 8-10 grams
- Fat: around 5-8 grams
- Carbohydrates: around 35-40 grams
- Fibre: around 5-8 grams

Please note that the nutritional information provided is an estimate and can vary depending on the specific ingredients and brands used.

Chapter 4: Dinner Recipes

Grilled chicken or turkey breast with roasted vegetables

Ingredients:

- 4-6 ounces grilled chicken or turkey breast
- Assorted vegetables (e.g., bell peppers, zucchini, onions, cherry tomatoes)
- Olive oil
- Salt and pepper to taste
- Herbs or spices of your choice (optional)

Instructions:

1. Preheat the oven to 400°F (200°C).
2. Toss the assorted vegetables with olive oil, salt, pepper, and any desired herbs or spices.
3. Lay the vegetables in a single layer on the baking sheet.

4. Roast the vegetables in the preheated oven for about 20-25 minutes or until they are tender and slightly browned.

5. Grill the chicken or turkey breast over medium-high heat for about 4-5 minutes per side or until it is cooked through.

6. Serve the grilled chicken or turkey breast with the roasted vegetables.

7. Enjoy.

<u>Nutritional Information</u>:

The nutritional content of grilled chicken or turkey breast with roasted vegetables can vary based on the specific quantities and types of ingredients used. Here is a general approximation per serving:

- Calories: around 250-300
- Protein: around 25-30 grams
- Fat: around 10-15 grams
- Carbohydrates: around 10-15 grams
- Fibre: around 5-8 grams

Baked salmon with quinoa and steamed greens

Ingredients:
- 4-6 ounces salmon fillet
- 1/2 cup cooked quinoa
- Assorted greens (e.g., spinach, kale, broccoli)
- Lemon juice
- Olive oil
- Salt and pepper to taste

Instructions:
1. Preheat the oven to 375°F (190°C).
2. Put the salmon fillet on top of a baking sheet lined with parchment paper.
3. Drizzle the salmon with lemon juice, olive oil, salt, and pepper.
4. Bake the salmon in the preheated oven for about 12-15 minutes or until it is cooked through and flakes easily with a fork.

5. While the salmon is baking, steam the assorted greens until they are tender.

6. Serve the baked salmon with the cooked quinoa and steamed greens.

7. Enjoy.

<u>Nutritional Information</u>:

The nutritional content of baked salmon with quinoa and steamed greens can vary based on the specific quantities and types of ingredients used. Here is a general approximation per serving:

- Calories: around 350-400
- Protein: around 25-30 grams
- Fat: around 15-20 grams
- Carbohydrates: around 20-25 grams
- Fibre: around 5-8 grams

Stir-fried tofu or shrimp with mixed vegetables

Ingredients:

- 4-6 ounces tofu or shrimp
- Assorted vegetables (e.g., broccoli, bell peppers, carrots, snap peas)
- Soy sauce or stir-fry sauce for seasoning
- Garlic and ginger (optional)
- Cooking oil

Instructions:

1. If using tofu, press it to remove excess moisture and cut it into cubes. If using shrimp, peel and devein them.
2. Heat a small amount of cooking oil in a large skillet or wok over medium-high heat.
3. If using garlic and ginger, sauté them in the hot oil until fragrant.
4. Add the tofu or shrimp to the skillet and cook until they are cooked through.

5. Add the assorted vegetables to the skillet and stir-fry until they are crisp-tender.

6. Drizzle soy sauce or stir-fry sauce over the stir-fry and toss to coat the ingredients evenly

7. Serve hot.

<u>Nutritional Information</u>:

The nutritional content of stir-fried tofu or shrimp with mixed vegetables can vary based on the specific quantities and types of ingredients used, as well as the sauce chosen. Here is a general approximation per serving:

- Calories: around 200-250
- Protein: around 15-20 grams
- Fat: around 8-10 grams
- Carbohydrates: around 15-20 grams
- Fibre: around 5-8 grams

Baked or grilled lean steak with sweet potato and grilled asparagus

Ingredients:
- 4-6 ounces lean steak (e.g., sirloin, tenderloin)
- 1 medium sweet potato
- 6-8 asparagus spears
- Olive oil
- Salt and pepper to taste
- Herbs or spices of your choice (optional)

Instructions:
1. If baking, preheat the oven to 400°F (200°C). If grilling, preheat the grill to medium-high heat.
2. Rub the steak with olive oil, salt, pepper, and any desired herbs or spices.
3. If baking, place the steak on a baking sheet lined with parchment paper. If grilling, place the steak directly on the grill grates.

4. Bake the steak in the preheated oven for about 10-15 minutes for medium-rare, or grill it for about 4-6 minutes per side for medium-rare.

5. While the steak is cooking, peel and cut the sweet potato into cubes. Place the sweet potato cubes on a baking sheet, drizzle with olive oil, sprinkle with salt and pepper, and roast in the oven for about 20-25 minutes or until they are tender and slightly browned.

6. Trim the woody ends of the asparagus spears. Drizzle the asparagus with olive oil, sprinkle it with salt and pepper, and grill them for about 5-7 minutes, turning occasionally, until they are tender and slightly charred.

7. Let the steak rest for a few minutes before slicing it against the grain.

8. Serve the baked or grilled steak with the roasted sweet potato and grilled asparagus.

9. Enjoy.

Nutritional Information:

The nutritional content of baked or grilled lean steak with sweet potato and grilled asparagus can vary based on the specific quantities and types of ingredients used. Here is a general approximation per serving:

- Calories: around 300-400
- Protein: around 25-30 grams
- Fat: around 10-15 grams
- Carbohydrates: around 20-25 grams
- Fibre: around 5-8 grams

Vegetable curry with cauliflower rice

Ingredients:
- Assorted vegetables (e.g., cauliflower, carrots, bell peppers, peas)
- Curry paste or powder
- Coconut milk
- Vegetable broth or water
- Olive oil
- Salt and pepper to taste

Instructions:

1. Cut the cauliflower into florets and pulse them in a food processor until they resemble rice.
2. In a large skillet or pot, heat a small amount of olive oil over medium heat.
3. Add the assorted vegetables to the skillet and cook until they are slightly softened.
4. Stir in the curry paste or powder, coating the vegetables evenly.
5. Add the coconut milk and vegetable broth or water to the skillet, and season with salt and pepper.
6. Bring the mixture to a simmer and let it cook for about 10-15 minutes, or until the vegetables are tender.
7. Serve the vegetable curry over the cauliflower rice.
8. Enjoy.

Nutritional Information:

The nutritional content of vegetable curry with cauliflower rice can vary based on

the specific quantities and types of ingredients used. Here is a general approximation per serving:

- Calories: around 200-250
- Protein: around 5-8 grams
- Fat: around 10-12 grams
- Carbohydrates: around 20-25 grams
- Fibre: around 8-10 grams

Zucchini noodles with lean ground turkey and tomato sauce

Ingredients:

- 1-2 medium zucchinis
- 4-6 ounces lean ground turkey
- Tomato sauce or marinara sauce
- Olive oil
- Garlic (optional)
- Salt and pepper to taste

Instructions:

1. Use a spiralizer or julienne peeler to create zucchini noodles from the zucchinis.

2. In a large skillet, heat a small amount of olive oil over medium heat.

3. If using garlic, sauté it in the hot oil until fragrant.

4. Add the lean ground turkey to the skillet and cook it until it is browned and cooked through.

5. Pour the tomato sauce or marinara sauce into the skillet and stir to combine with the ground turkey. Simmer the sauce for a few minutes until heated through.

6. Add the zucchini noodles to the skillet and cook for about 2-3 minutes, or until they are slightly softened.

7. Season with salt and pepper to taste.

8. Serve the zucchini noodles with the lean ground turkey and tomato sauce.

9. Enjoy.

Nutritional Information:

The nutritional content of zucchini noodles with lean ground turkey and tomato sauce can vary based on the specific quantities and types of ingredients used. Here is a general approximation per serving:

- Calories: around 200-250
- Protein: around 15-20 grams

- Fat: around 8-10 grams

- Carbohydrates: around 15-20 grams

- Fibre: around 5-8 grams

Grilled shrimp or chicken skewers with mixed salad

Ingredients:

- 4-6 ounces shrimp or chicken breast, cut into cubes
- Assorted vegetables (e.g., lettuce, tomatoes, cucumbers, onions)
- Lemon juice
- Olive oil
- Salt and pepper to taste
- Skewers for grilling

Instructions:

1. If using wooden skewers, soak them in water for about 30 minutes before grilling to prevent burning.
2. Thread the shrimp or chicken cubes onto the skewers.

3. Preheat the grill to medium-high heat.

4. Grill the skewers for about 4-6 minutes per side, or until the shrimp is pink and cooked through, or the chicken is cooked through and no longer pink in the centre.

5. Meanwhile, prepare the mixed salad by combining the assorted vegetables in a bowl.

6. Drizzle lemon juice and olive oil over the salad, and season with salt and pepper.

7. Toss the salad to coat the vegetables evenly.

8. Serve the grilled shrimp or chicken skewers with the mixed salad.

9. Enjoy.

Nutritional Information:

The nutritional content of grilled shrimp or chicken skewers with mixed salad can vary based on the specific quantities and types of ingredients used. Here is a general approximation per serving:

- Calories: around 200-250
- Protein: around 20-25 grams
- Fat: around 8-10 grams

- Carbohydrates: around 10-15 grams
- Fibre: around 5-8 grams

Baked cod or halibut with steamed vegetables

Ingredients:
- 4-6 ounces cod or halibut fillet
- Assorted vegetables (e.g., broccoli, carrots, cauliflower)
- Lemon juice
- Olive oil
- Salt and pepper to taste

Instructions:
1. Preheat the oven to 375°F (190°C).
2. Place the cod or halibut fillet on a baking sheet lined with parchment paper.
3. Drizzle the fish with lemon juice, olive oil, salt, and pepper.

4. Bake the fish in the preheated oven for about 12-15 minutes or until it is cooked through and flakes easily with a fork.

5. While the fish is baking, steam the assorted vegetables until they are tender.

6. Serve the baked cod or halibut with the steamed vegetables.

7. Enjoy.

Nutritional Information:

The nutritional content of baked cod or halibut with steamed vegetables can vary based on the specific quantities and types of ingredients used. Here is a general approximation per serving:

- Calories: around 200-250
- Protein: around 20-25 grams
- Fat: around 5-8 grams
- Carbohydrates: around 10-15 grams
- Fibre: around 5-8 grams

Turkey or chicken chilli

Ingredients:
- 4-6 ounces ground turkey or chicken
- 1 can diced tomatoes
- 1 can kidney beans, drained and rinsed
- Assorted vegetables (e.g., onions, bell peppers, carrots)
- Chili powder
- Cumin
- Garlic powder
- Salt and pepper to taste

Instructions:
1. In a large pot, cook the ground turkey or chicken over medium heat until it is browned and cooked through.
2. Add the assorted vegetables to the pot and cook until they are slightly softened.
3. Stir in the diced tomatoes, kidney beans, chilli powder, cumin, garlic powder, salt, and pepper.

4. Bring the mixture to a boil, then reduce the heat to low and let it simmer for about 20-30 minutes, stirring occasionally.

5. Taste and adjust the seasonings as needed.

6. Serve the turkey or chicken chilli hot.

7. Enjoy.

<u>Nutritional Information:</u>

The nutritional content of turkey or chicken chilli can vary based on the specific quantities and types of ingredients used. Here is a general approximation per serving:

- Calories: around 200-250
- Protein: around 15-20 grams
- Fat: around 5-8 grams
- Carbohydrates: around 20-25 grams
- Fibre: around 8-10 grams

Stuffed bell peppers with lean ground beef or turkey

Ingredients:
- 2-3 bell peppers
- 4-6 ounces lean ground beef or turkey
- Assorted vegetables (e.g., onions, tomatoes, corn)
- Cooked rice or quinoa
- Tomato sauce or marinara sauce
- Olive oil
- Salt and pepper to taste
- Shredded cheese (optional)

Instructions:
1. Preheat the oven to 375°F (190°C).
2. Cut off the top of the bell peppers and remove the membranes and seeds.
3. In a large skillet, heat a small amount of olive oil over medium heat.
4. Add the lean ground beef or turkey to the skillet and cook it until it is browned and cooked through.

5. Add the assorted vegetables to the skillet and cook until they are slightly softened.

6. Stir in the cooked rice or quinoa and tomato sauce or marinara sauce. Season with salt and pepper to taste.

7. Fill each bell pepper with the ground beef or turkey mixture.

8. If desired, sprinkle shredded cheese on top of the stuffed bell peppers.

9. Place the stuffed bell peppers in a baking dish and bake in the preheated oven for about 25-30 minutes or until the peppers are tender and the cheese is melted and bubbly.

10. Serve the stuffed bell peppers hot.

11. Enjoy.

Nutritional Information:

The nutritional content of stuffed bell peppers with lean ground beef or turkey can vary based on the specific quantities and types of ingredients used. Here is a general approximation per serving:

- Calories: around 250-300
- Protein: around 20-25 grams

- Fat: around 8-10 grams

- Carbohydrates: around 20-25 grams

- Fibre: around 5-8 grams

Chapter 5: Snacks and Treats

Here are ten snack and treat options suitable for men with type 1 diabetes:

Apple slices with natural peanut butter:

Ingredients:
- 1 apple
- Natural peanut butter (without hydrogenated oils or added sugar)

Instructions:
1. Wash and slice the apple into thin wedges.
2. Serve the apple slices with a side of natural peanut butter for dipping.
3. Enjoy!

Nutritional Information:

The nutritional content can vary depending on the size of the apple and the amount of peanut butter used. Here is a general approximation for a medium-sized apple (approximately 154 grams) and 2 tablespoons of natural peanut butter:

- Calories: around 200-250
- Protein: around 6-8 grams
- Fat: around 10-12 grams
- Carbohydrates: around 25-30 grams
- Fibre: around 5-8 grams

Greek yoghurt with berries

Ingredients:

- Greek yoghurt (unsweetened)
- Assorted berries (e.g., strawberries, blueberries, raspberries)

Instructions:

1. Place a desired amount of Greek yoghurt in a bowl.
2. Wash and add the assorted berries on top of the Greek yoghurt.
3. Mix well or enjoy layered.
4. Optional: Add a sprinkle of nuts or seeds for added texture and nutrition.
5. Enjoy!

Nutritional Information:

The nutritional content can vary based on the specific quantities and types of ingredients used. Here is a general approximation for 1 cup of Greek yoghourt (245 grams) and 1 cup of assorted berries (approximately 140 grams):

- Calories: around 150-200
- Protein: around 15-20 grams
- Fat: around 0-5 grams
- Carbohydrates: around 20-25 grams
- Fibre: around 5-8 grams

Hard-boiled eggs

Ingredients:

- Eggs

Instructions:

1. Place the eggs in a saucepan and add enough water to cover them.
2. Boil the water over medium or high heat.
3. Once the water reaches a rolling boil, reduce the heat to low and let the eggs simmer for about 9-12 minutes.
4. Remove the eggs from the heat and transfer them to a bowl of ice water to cool and stop the cooking process.
5. Once cooled, peel the eggs and they are ready to eat.
6. Enjoy!

Nutritional Information:

The nutritional content can vary slightly based on the size of the eggs. Here is a general approximation for a large-sized egg (approximately 50 grams):

- Calories: around 70-80
- Protein: around 6 grams

- Fat: around 5 grams
- Carbohydrates: around 0 grams
- Fibre: around 0 grams

Veggie sticks with hummus

Ingredients:
- Assorted vegetables (e.g., carrots, celery, bell peppers, cucumber)
- Hummus

Instructions:
1. Wash and cut the vegetables into sticks or bite-sized pieces.
2. Serve the veggie sticks with a side of hummus for dipping.
3. Enjoy!

Nutritional Information:

The nutritional content can vary based on the specific quantities and types of vegetables used and the portion size of hummus. Here is a general approximation for a serving size of about 1 cup of assorted vegetables (approximately 125 grams) and 2 tablespoons of hummus:

- Calories: around 100-150
- Protein: around 3-5 grams
- Fat: around 5-8 grams
- Carbohydrates: around 15-20 grams
- Fibre: around 5-8 grams

Nuts and seeds

Ingredients:
- Assorted nuts (e.g., almonds, walnuts, cashews)
- Assorted seeds (e.g., pumpkin seeds, sunflower seeds, chia seeds)

Instructions:

1. Combine a handful of assorted nuts and seeds in a bowl.
2. Mix well to create your desired blend.
3. Enjoy the nuts and seeds as a snack or add them to other dishes for extra crunch and nutrition.
4. Enjoy!

Nutritional Information:

The nutritional content can vary based on the specific quantities and types of nuts and seeds used. Here is a general approximation for a serving size of about 1 ounce (28 grams) of mixed nuts and seeds:

- Calories: around 150-200
- Protein: around 5-8 grams
- Fat: around 10-15 grams
- Carbohydrates: around 5-10 grams
- Fibre: around 3-5 grams

Cheese and whole grain crackers

Ingredients:

- Cheese (e.g., cheddar, Swiss, mozzarella)
- Whole grain crackers

Instructions:

1. Cut the cheese into bite-sized pieces or slices.
2. Serve the cheese with a side of whole grain crackers.
3. Enjoy!

Nutritional Information:

The nutritional content can vary based on the specific quantities and types of cheese and crackers used. Here is a general approximation for a serving size of about 1 ounce (28 grams) of cheese and 4-6 whole grain crackers:

- Calories: around 150-200
- Protein: around 7-9 grams
- Fat: around 10-12 grams
- Carbohydrates: around 10-15 grams

- Fibre: around 2-4 grams

Cottage cheese with cherry tomatoes

Ingredients:
- Cottage cheese (low-fat or regular)
- Cherry tomatoes

Instructions:
1. Wash and cut the cherry tomatoes into halves or quarters.
2. Place the desired amount of cottage cheese in a bowl.
3. Add the cherry tomatoes on top of the cottage cheese.
4. Mix well or enjoy layered.
5. Optional: Season with salt, pepper, or herbs for added flavour.
6. Enjoy!

Nutritional Information:

The nutritional content can vary based on the specific quantities and types of ingredients used. Here is a general approximation for 1/2 cup (113 grams) of cottage cheese and 1 cup (150 grams) of cherry tomatoes:

- Calories: around 100-150
- Protein: around 15-20 grams
- Fat: around 0-5 grams
- Carbohydrates: around 10-15 grams
- Fibre: around 2-4 grams

Turkey or chicken roll-ups

Ingredients:
- Turkey or chicken slices (lean, deli-style)
- Assorted vegetables (e.g., lettuce, cucumber, bell peppers)
- Condiments (e.g., mustard, mayonnaise, hummus)

Instructions:

1. Lay the turkey or chicken slices flat on a clean surface.
2. Place a layer of assorted vegetables on top of the turkey or chicken slices.
3. Add a small amount of condiments, such as mustard, mayonnaise, or hummus, if desired.
4. Roll up the turkey or chicken slices tightly to form a roll-up.
5. Secure the roll-up with toothpicks if necessary.
6. Enjoy!

Nutritional Information:

The nutritional content can vary based on the specific quantities and types of ingredients used. Here is a general approximation for a serving size of 2-3 slices of turkey or chicken (approximately 60 grams) and a variety of vegetables and condiments:

- Calories: around 100-150
- Protein: around 15-20 grams
- Fat: around 0-5 grams
- Carbohydrates: around 2-5 grams
- Fibre: around 0-2 grams

Roasted chickpeas

Ingredients:
- Canned chickpeas
- Olive oil
- Seasonings (e.g., salt, pepper, paprika, cumin, garlic powder)

Instructions:
1. Preheat the oven to 400°F (200°C).
2. Rinse and drain the canned chickpeas.
3. Put the chickpeas on top of a baking sheet lined with parchment paper.
4. Drizzle the chickpeas with olive oil and season with desired seasonings.
5. Toss the chickpeas to ensure they are evenly coated with oil and seasonings.
6. Roast the chickpeas in the preheated oven for about 25-30 minutes, or until they are crispy and golden brown.

7. Remove from the oven and let them cool slightly before serving.

8. Enjoy!

Nutritional Information:

The nutritional content can vary based on the specific quantities and types of ingredients used. Here is a general approximation for a serving size of about 1/2 cup (82 grams) of roasted chickpeas:

- Calories: around 120-150
- Protein: around 6-8 grams
- Fat: around 2-4 grams
- Carbohydrates: around 20-25 grams
- Fibre: around 5-8 grams

Dark chocolate-covered almonds:

Ingredients:

- Dark chocolate (70% cocoa or higher)
- Almonds (raw or roasted)

Instructions:

1. Melt the dark chocolate using a double boiler or microwave, stirring until smooth.
2. Dip each almond into the melted chocolate, coating it entirely.
3. Put the chocolate-covered almonds on top of the baking sheet lined with parchment paper.
4. Allow the chocolate to harden by placing the baking sheet in the refrigerator for about 30 minutes.
5. Once the chocolate is set, remove the almonds from the baking sheet.
6. Enjoy!

Nutritional Information:

The nutritional content can vary based on the specific quantities and types of ingredients used. Here is a general approximation for a serving size of about 1 ounce (28 grams) of dark chocolate-covered almonds:

- Calories: around 150-200
- Protein: around 3-5 grams
- Fat: around 10-12 grams

- Carbohydrates: around 10-15 grams
- Fibre: around 2-4 grams

Chapter 6: Meal Planning Tips and Tricks

14-Day Meal plan

Here's a 14-day meal plan for men with type 1 diabetes. Each day includes breakfast, lunch, dinner, and snacks. This meal plan focuses on balanced meals that incorporate lean proteins, fibre-rich carbohydrates, and healthy fats.

Day 1:

Breakfast: Greek Yoghourt with Mixed Berries
- Combine Greek yoghurt and mixed berries. Enjoy!

Snack: Hard-Boiled Egg
- Boil an egg until hard-boiled. Peel and enjoy.
Lunch: Grilled Chicken Salad together with Vegetables and Mixed Greens.
- Grill chicken breast. Slice and combine with mixed greens and vegetables. Add dressing. Toss and enjoy.

Snack: Carrot Sticks with Hummus

- Cut carrot sticks. Serve with hummus. Enjoy.

Dinner: Baked Salmon with Quinoa and Roasted Asparagus

- Season salmon. Bake. Cook quinoa. Toss asparagus with oil, salt, and pepper. Roast. Plate and enjoy together.

Day 2:

Breakfast: Spinach and Mushroom Omelette

- Make an omelette with spinach and mushrooms. Enjoy!

Snack: Greek Yoghourt with Almonds

- Combine Greek yoghurt with almonds. Enjoy!

Lunch: Turkey and Vegetable Stir-Fry with Brown Rice

- Stir-fry turkey and vegetables. Serve with brown rice. Enjoy!

Snack: Celery Sticks with Almond Butter

- Serve celery sticks with almond butter. Enjoy!

Dinner: Grilled Chicken Breast with Roasted Brussels Sprouts and Sweet Potatoes
- Grill chicken breast. Roast Brussels sprouts and sweet potatoes. Serve together. Enjoy!

Day 3:

Breakfast: Overnight Oats with Berries
- Prepare overnight oats with berries. Enjoy!

Snack: Cottage Cheese with Sliced Tomatoes
- Serve cottage cheese with sliced tomatoes. Enjoy!

Lunch: Grilled Shrimp Salad with Quinoa
- Grill shrimp. Prepare a salad with quinoa. Combine and enjoy!

Snack: Apple Slices with Almond Butter
- Slice an apple. Serve with almond butter. Enjoy!

Dinner: Grilled Lean Steak with Roasted Asparagus and Quinoa

- Grill lean steak. Roast asparagus. Prepare quinoa. Serve together. Enjoy!

Day 4:

Breakfast: Veggie and Cheese Omelette with Whole-Grain Toast

- Make a veggie and cheese omelette. Serve with whole-grain toast.

Snack: Mixed Nuts

- Enjoy a handful of mixed nuts as a snack.

Lunch: Tuna Salad Lettuce Wraps

- Prepare tuna salad. Use lettuce leaves as wraps. Enjoy!

Snack: Roasted Chickpeas

- Roast chickpeas. Enjoy them as a snack.

Dinner: Baked Cod with Lemon Herb Sauce, Quinoa, and Steamed Green Beans

- Bake cod with lemon herb sauce. Serve with quinoa and steamed green beans. Enjoy!

Day 5:

Breakfast: Chia Seed Pudding with Berries
- Make chia seed pudding. Top with berries. Enjoy!

Snack: Celery Sticks with Cream Cheese
- Serve celery sticks with cream cheese. Enjoy!

Lunch: Grilled Vegetable Wrap with Whole Wheat Tortilla
- Grill vegetables. Fill a whole wheat tortilla with grilled vegetables. Enjoy the wrap!

Snack: Cottage Cheese with Sliced Peaches
- Serve cottage cheese with sliced peaches. Enjoy!

Dinner: Baked Chicken Thighs with Roasted Cauliflower and Steamed Broccoli
- Bake chicken thighs. Roast cauliflower. Steam broccoli. Serve together. Enjoy!

Day 6:

Breakfast: Vegetable Omelette with Whole-Grain Toast
- Make a vegetable omelette. Serve with whole-grain toast.

Snack: Greek Yoghourt with Walnuts and Honey
- Combine Greek yoghurt, walnuts, and a drizzle of honey. Enjoy!

Lunch: Quinoa Salad with Grilled Chicken and Mixed Vegetables
- Prepare a quinoa salad with grilled chicken and mixed vegetables. Enjoy!

Snack: Cucumber Slices with Smoked Salmon
- Serve cucumber slices with smoked salmon. Enjoy!

Dinner: Lean Beef Stir-Fry with Brown Rice
- Make a lean beef stir-fry. Serve with brown rice. Enjoy!

Day 7:

Breakfast: Overnight Chia Oats with Almond Butter and Banana
- Prepare overnight chia oats. Top with almond butter and sliced banana. Enjoy!

Snack: Cherry Tomatoes with Mozzarella Cheese
- Serve cherry tomatoes with mozzarella cheese. Enjoy!

Lunch: Grilled Shrimp and Avocado Salad
- Grill shrimp. Prepare a salad with avocado. Combine and enjoy!

Snack: Almond and Coconut Energy Balls
- Make almond and coconut energy balls. Enjoy as a snack.

Dinner: Baked Chicken Breast with Roasted Root Vegetables
- Bake chicken breast. Roast root vegetables. Serve together. Enjoy!

Day 8:

Breakfast: Scrambled Eggs with Spinach and Feta Cheese
- Make scrambled eggs with spinach and feta cheese. Enjoy!

Snack: Sliced Bell Peppers with Guacamole
- Serve sliced bell peppers with guacamole. Enjoy!

Lunch: Black Bean Salad and Quinoa together with Grilled Chicken
- Prepare a quinoa and black bean salad. Add grilled chicken. Enjoy!

Snack: Greek Yoghourt with Cinnamon

- Serve Greek yoghurt with a sprinkle of cinnamon. Enjoy!

Dinner: Baked Tofu with Stir-Fried Vegetables and Brown Rice
- Bake tofu. Stir-fry vegetables. Serve with brown rice. Enjoy!

Day 9:

Breakfast: Whole Grain Toast with Smoked Salmon and Avocado.
- Toast whole grain bread. Top with avocado and smoked salmon. Enjoy!

Snack: Baby Carrots with Hummus
- Serve baby carrots with hummus. Enjoy!

Lunch: Avocado Wrap and Turkey together with Whole Wheat Tortilla
- Fill a whole wheat tortilla with turkey and avocado. Roll it up to make a wrap. Enjoy!

Snack: Handful of Almonds
- Grab a handful of almonds and enjoy as a snack.

Dinner: Roasted Brussels Sprouts together with Grilled Salmon and Quinoa
- Grill salmon. Roast Brussels sprouts. Prepare quinoa. Serve together. Enjoy!

Day 10:

Breakfast: Oatmeal with Sliced Bananas and Honey
- Cook oatmeal. Top with sliced bananas. Drizzle with honey. Enjoy!

Snack: Hard-Boiled Eggs with Salt and Pepper
- Prepare hard-boiled eggs. Sprinkle it with pepper and a pinch of salt. Enjoy!

Lunch: Chicken and Vegetable Kebabs with Side Salad
- Skewer chicken and vegetables. Grill or bake until cooked. Serve with a side salad. Enjoy!

Snack: Fresh Berries with Greek Yoghourt
- Serve fresh berries with a dollop of Greek yoghurt. Enjoy!

Dinner: Lean Ground Turkey Chili with Mixed Vegetables
- Cook lean ground turkey with chilli seasonings. Add mixed vegetables. Simmer until cooked. Enjoy the turkey chilli with mixed vegetables.

Day 11:

Breakfast: Veggie Scramble with Mushrooms, Bell Peppers and Onions
- Prepare a veggie scramble with bell peppers, onions, and mushrooms. Enjoy!

Snack: Apple Slices with Peanut Butter
- Slice an apple. Serve with a tablespoon of peanut butter. Enjoy!

Lunch: Spinach and Feta Stuffed Chicken Breast with Quinoa
- Stuff chicken breast with spinach and feta. Cook until chicken is done. Serve with quinoa. Enjoy!

Snack: Roasted Edamame
- Roast edamame until crispy. Enjoy as a snack.

Dinner: Baked Cod with Roasted Cherry Tomatoes and Steamed Asparagus
- Bake cod. Roast cherry tomatoes. Steam asparagus. Serve together. Enjoy!

Day 12:

Breakfast: Smoothie Bowl with Mixed Berries, Spinach, and Almond Milk
- Blend mixed berries, spinach, and almond milk. Pour into a bowl. Enjoy as a smoothie bowl.

Snack: Cottage Cheese with Sliced Peaches
- Serve cottage cheese with sliced peaches. Enjoy!

Lunch: Quinoa and Vegetable Stir-Fry with Tofu
- Cook quinoa. Stir-fry vegetables and tofu. Combine with cooked quinoa. Enjoy!

Snack: Celery Sticks with Almond Butter
- Serve celery sticks with almond butter. Enjoy!

Dinner: Grilled Chicken Skewers with Bell Peppers and Onions, served with Brown Rice
- Skewer chicken, bell peppers, and onions. Grill until cooked. Serve with cooked brown rice. Enjoy!

Day 13:

Breakfast: Greek Yoghurt Parfait with Fresh Berries and Granola
- Layer Greek yoghurt, granola, and fresh berries in a bowl. Enjoy!

Snack: Trail Mix with Dried Fruits Nuts and Seeds
- Combine nuts, seeds, and dried fruits to make a trail mix. Enjoy as a snack.

Lunch: Shrimp and Vegetable Stir-Fry with Cauliflower Rice
- Stir-fry shrimp and vegetables. Serve with cauliflower rice. Enjoy!

Snack: Cucumber Slices with Tzatziki Dip
- Slice cucumbers. Serve with tzatziki dip. Enjoy!

Dinner: Baked Turkey Meatballs with Marinara Sauce and Zucchini Noodles
- Prepare turkey meatballs and bake them. Serve with zucchini noodles and marinara sauce. Enjoy!

Day 14:

Breakfast: Breakfast Burrito with Scrambled Eggs, Black Beans, and Salsa
- Make scrambled eggs. Warm up black beans and salsa. Wrap the eggs, beans, and salsa in a whole wheat tortilla to make a breakfast burrito.

Snack: Mixed Nuts and Dried Fruits

- Combine mixed nuts and dried fruits. Enjoy as a snack.

Lunch: Grilled Vegetable and Goat Cheese Salad with Balsamic Vinaigrette
- Grill vegetables. Combine with goat cheese. Drizzle with balsamic vinaigrette to make a salad.

Snack: Rice Cakes with Almond Butter
- Spread almond butter on rice cakes. Enjoy as a snack.

Dinner: Baked Chicken Breast with Steamed Broccoli and Roasted Sweet Potatoes
- Bake chicken breast. Roast sweet potatoes. Steam broccoli. Serve together. Enjoy!

Conclusion

Putting It All Together: A Balanced Approach to Type 1

Managing type 1 diabetes necessitates a complete and balanced strategy that includes nutrition, exercise, medication, and overall lifestyle choices. Here's how to put it all together to manage type 1 diabetes effectively:

1. Diabetes Education: Through education, you can gain a firm understanding of diabetes management. Discover carbohydrate counting, insulin delivery, blood sugar monitoring, and the effects of various foods on blood sugar levels. To improve your knowledge, attend diabetes education seminars or work with a certified diabetes educator.

2. Eating Well: Eat a well-balanced diet rich in entire, nutrient-dense foods. Include non-starchy veggies, lean meats, healthy fats, and complex carbohydrates in your

diet. To properly regulate blood sugar levels, practice portion management, carbohydrate counting, and glycemic index/load awareness. Include fibre-rich foods in your diet to maintain stable blood sugar levels and proper digestion.

3. Regular Physical Activity: Engage in regular physical activity that involves cardiovascular workouts (such as brisk walking, swimming, or cycling) as well as strength training exercises. Each week, aim for at least 150 minutes of moderate-intensity aerobic activity, as well as two or more days of strength training. Consult your healthcare professional to determine the right intensity and duration of exercise depending on your unique needs.

4. Medication Management: Stick to your medication routine, which may include insulin delivery or other diabetes drugs. Under the supervision of your healthcare professional, monitor your blood sugar levels regularly and modify your medication as needed.

5. Blood Sugar Monitoring: Use a glucose metre or a continuous glucose monitoring (CGM) device to check your blood sugar levels regularly. This enables you to comprehend how various diets, activities, and lifestyle factors affect your blood sugar levels. Make informed decisions about your food, exercise, and medication modifications using the information provided.

6. Stress Management: Use stress-reduction tactics to lessen the influence of stress on your blood sugar levels. Engage in relaxing and unwinding activities such as meditation, deep breathing exercises, yoga, or hobbies. Make time for self-care and hobbies that offer you joy and tranquillity.

7. Schedule regular check-ups with your healthcare team, which should include your endocrinologist, diabetes educator, and other experts as needed. It is critical to evaluate your overall health regularly, including blood pressure, cholesterol levels, renal function, and eye health, to recognize and manage any potential concerns early.

8. Emotional assistance: Seek emotional assistance from friends, relatives, or support groups who are familiar with the difficulties of living with type 1 diabetes. Consider joining diabetes support groups or online forums where you may share your experiences, get support, and learn new things.

9. Lifestyle adjustments: Make good lifestyle adjustments that will help you manage your diabetes. Get enough sleep, limit your alcohol use, avoid smoking, and keep a healthy weight. These lifestyle decisions have the potential to have a substantial impact on your general health and blood sugar control.

10. Regular Self-Assessment: Evaluate your diabetes management regularly. Determine what is working well and what needs to be improved. Maintain a balanced and effective strategy for treating your type 1 diabetes by staying motivated and making modifications as needed.

Remember that everyone's diabetes management plan will differ, so it's critical to collaborate with your healthcare provider to develop an individualised strategy that meets your personal needs and goals. You can effectively manage type 1 diabetes and live a fulfilling and healthy life by taking a balanced approach that includes good food, frequent exercise, adequate medication management, and general self-care.

Staying Motivated and Inspired

Maintaining a positive outlook and properly caring for your health requires staying motivated and inspired while managing type 1 diabetes. Here are some methods for staying motivated on your diabetes journey:

1. Set Meaningful Goals: Set specific and attainable goals for your diabetes management. Having clear goals, whether it's achieving target blood sugar levels, incorporating regular exercise into your routine, or trying new healthy recipes, can provide a feeling of purpose and direction.

2. Recognize and Celebrate Small Accomplishments: Recognize and celebrate minor accomplishments along the road. Every step you take toward better diabetes management is a victory worth celebrating. Reward yourself for achieving milestones by treating yourself to something you appreciate or participating in a favourite activity.

3. Find Help: Surround yourself with a strong support network. Connect with other people who have type 1 diabetes by joining support organisations, online communities, or attending local meet-ups. Sharing experiences, problems, and accomplishments with like-minded people can bring motivation, inspiration, and a sense of belonging.

4. Educate Yourself: Keep up to date on the newest advances and research in diabetes treatment. Attend diabetes-related seminars, workshops, or webinars. Knowledge enables you to make informed health decisions and encourages a proactive approach to treating your disease.

5. Maintain a good Attitude: Maintain a good attitude and concentrate on the things you can manage. Try not to concentrate on defeats or negative ideas. Self-compassion is important, as is remembering that controlling type 1 diabetes is a journey with ups and downs. Positive affirmations or inspirational quotes that uplift and motivate you should be all around you.

6. document Your Progress: Keep a notebook or use a mobile app to document your blood sugar readings, meals, exercise, and other diabetes-related aspects. Seeing your progress over time can be motivational and can reveal patterns or areas for growth.

7. Practice Self-Care: Make self-care activities that nourish your mind, body, and spirit a priority. This could involve participating in hobbies, practising relaxing techniques, getting proper sleep, or spending time outside in nature. Taking care of your general well-being improves your ability to effectively manage diabetes.

8. Experiment with New techniques: Try new techniques or technologies to keep your diabetes management

routine fresh and entertaining. You may, for example, try out alternative workout routines, try out new healthy recipes, or think about utilising a continuous glucose monitoring (CGM) device. Accepting change and figuring out what works best for you can rekindle motivation and passion.

9. Seek Professional Advice: Meet with your healthcare team frequently and seek advice from your healthcare practitioner, certified dietitian, or diabetes educator. They can provide you with personalised guidance, answer your questions, and assist you in sticking to your diabetes control plan.

10. Visualise Your Health Goals: Imagine how good diabetes management would improve your entire health and well-being. To visualise yourself having a vibrant, healthy life, make a vision board or employ visualisation techniques. Visual reminders might assist you in remaining focused and inspired on your trip.

Remember that motivation can change, and it's common to face obstacles along the path. Be patient with yourself, practice self-compassion, and draw strength from your accomplishments thus far. You may stay motivated, inspired, and empowered to live your best life with type 1 diabetes by adopting these methods into your diabetes care practice.

You got this

	Breakfast	Lunch	Dinner
Monday			

	Breakfast	Lunch	Dinner
Tuesday			

	Breakfast	Lunch	Dinner
Wednesday			

	Breakfast	Lunch	Dinner
Thursday			

	Breakfast	Lunch	Dinner
Friday			

	Breakfast	Lunch	Dinner
Saturday			

	Breakfast	Lunch	Dinner
Sunday			

	Breakfast	Lunch	Dinner
Monday			
Tuesday			
Wednesday			
Thursday			
Friday			
Saturday			
Sunday			

FOOD JOURNAL

Breakfast   Servings   Calories

	Servings	Calories
		Subtotal

Snack

	Servings	Calories
		Subtotal

Lunch

	Servings	Calories
		Subtotal

Snack

	Servings	Calories
		Subtotal

Dinner

	Servings	Calories
		Subtotal

Snack

	Servings	Calories
		Subtotal

Total Calories From Food ☐

FITNESS ACTIVITY JOURNAL

	Duration	Calories

Total Calories From Fitness ☐

NOTES

FOOD JOURNAL

Breakfast   Servings   Calories

	Servings	Calories
	Subtotal	

Snack

	Servings	Calories
	Subtotal	

Lunch

	Servings	Calories
	Subtotal	

Snack

	Servings	Calories
	Subtotal	

Dinner

	Servings	Calories
	Subtotal	

Snack

	Servings	Calories
	Subtotal	

Total Calories From Food _____

FITNESS ACTIVITY JOURNAL

	Duration	Calories

Total Calories From Fitness _____

NOTES

_____
_____
_____
_____
_____
_____

FOOD JOURNAL

Breakfast Servings Calories

	Subtotal	

Snack

	Subtotal	

Lunch

	Subtotal	

Snack

	Subtotal	

Dinner

	Subtotal	

Snack

	Subtotal	

Total Calories From Food

FITNESS ACTIVITY JOURNAL

Duration Calories

Total Calories From Fitness

NOTES

Weekly Diabetes Record

Name: _____

Date:	Breakfast	Snack	Lunch	Snack	Dinner	Snack	Bedtime	Night	Notes
Blood Sugar									
Insulin Dose									
Grams Carb									
Activity									

Date:	Breakfast	Snack	Lunch	Snack	Dinner	Snack	Bedtime	Night	Notes
Blood Sugar									
Insulin Dose									
Grams Carb									
Activity									

Date:	Breakfast	Snack	Lunch	Snack	Dinner	Snack	Bedtime	Night	Notes
Blood Sugar									
Insulin Dose									
Grams Carb									
Activity									

Date:	Breakfast	Snack	Lunch	Snack	Dinner	Snack	Bedtime	Night	Notes
Blood Sugar									
Insulin Dose									
Grams Carb									
Activity									

Date:	Breakfast	Snack	Lunch	Snack	Dinner	Snack	Bedtime	Night	Notes
Blood Sugar									
Insulin Dose									
Grams Carb									
Activity									

Date:	Breakfast	Snack	Lunch	Snack	Dinner	Snack	Bedtime	Night	Notes
Blood Sugar									
Insulin Dose									
Grams Carb									
Activity									

Date:	Breakfast	Snack	Lunch	Snack	Dinner	Snack	Bedtime	Night	Notes
Blood Sugar									
Insulin Dose									
Grams Carb									
Activity									

Weekly Diabetes Record

Name: _____

Date:	Breakfast	Snack	Lunch	Snack	Dinner	Snack	Bedtime	Night	Notes
Blood Sugar									
Insulin Dose									
Grams Carb									
Activity									

Date:	Breakfast	Snack	Lunch	Snack	Dinner	Snack	Bedtime	Night	Notes
Blood Sugar									
Insulin Dose									
Grams Carb									
Activity									

Date:	Breakfast	Snack	Lunch	Snack	Dinner	Snack	Bedtime	Night	Notes
Blood Sugar									
Insulin Dose									
Grams Carb									
Activity									

Date:	Breakfast	Snack	Lunch	Snack	Dinner	Snack	Bedtime	Night	Notes
Blood Sugar									
Insulin Dose									
Grams Carb									
Activity									

Date:	Breakfast	Snack	Lunch	Snack	Dinner	Snack	Bedtime	Night	Notes
Blood Sugar									
Insulin Dose									
Grams Carb									
Activity									

Date:	Breakfast	Snack	Lunch	Snack	Dinner	Snack	Bedtime	Night	Notes
Blood Sugar									
Insulin Dose									
Grams Carb									
Activity									

Date:	Breakfast	Snack	Lunch	Snack	Dinner	Snack	Bedtime	Night	Notes
Blood Sugar									
Insulin Dose									
Grams Carb									
Activity									

Made in the USA
Monee, IL
13 April 2024